Pneumatic Antiphonal

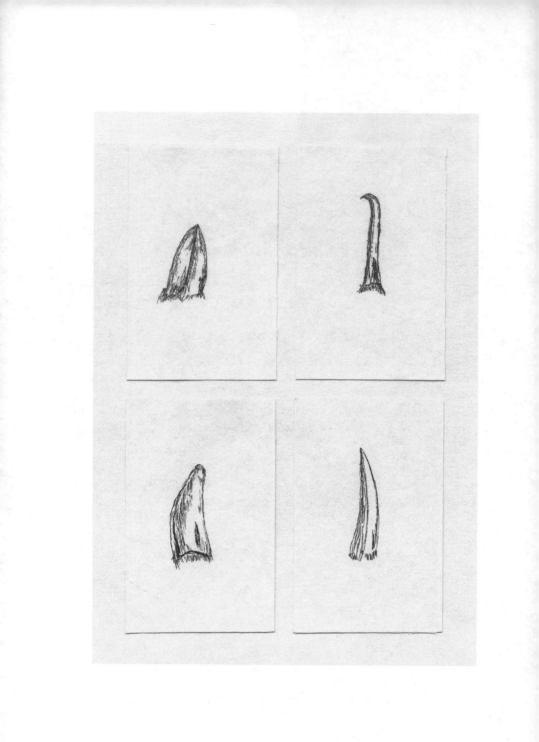

Sylvia Legris

Pneumatic Antiphonal

NEW DIRECTIONS POETRY PAMPHLET #4

The illustrations are by the author.

Cover design by Office of Paul Sahre
Interior design by Erik Rieselbach
Manufactured in the United States of America
New Directions Books are printed on acid-free paper
First published as New Directions Poetry Pamphlet #4 in 2013
Published simultaneously in Canada by Penguin Books Canada Limited

Library of Congress Cataloging-in-Publication Data
Legris, Sylvia.
Pneumatic Antiphonal / Sylvia Legris.
p. cm. — (A New Directions Poetry Pamphlet ; #4)
ISBN 978-0-8112-2040-8 (paperbook : acid-free paper)
I. Title.
PR9199.3.L3945P64 2013
811'.54—dc23

                    2012040748

10 9 8 7 6 5 4 3 2 1

New Directions Books are published for James Laughlin
by New Directions Publishing Corporation
80 Eighth Avenue, New York, NY 10011

Lore: 1 (premise)

The theory of corpuscular flight is the cardinal premise of red birds carrying song-particles carrying oxygen. Erythrocytic. Sticky. Five quarts of migration.

Lore: 2 (decoy)

1

Historiated hiss alarms and *Zeet!* whistles. The first note inter-
woven with reed and rectrices. Intervertevibrato. Interstitial
pishing. An onomatopoeic anatomy.

2

Bird the bilateral lung field. Downwind. (Catarrhic.) The
bronchial understory couched in Creeping Spikerush, Three-
square bulrush. Emargination and notch. Sternal notch. Costal
facets.

3

chideep chidideep chideep chidideep... Call epiglottal. Call Swallow.
Flight-sing the oscinic; the suboscinic, the supra-. (Oxygen
song. H_2O song. Ozonic.)

Lore: 3 (midrib nidifying)

1

Airway edifice. Feather-compound composite. The leaf-shaped epiglottis (petiolated, parallel-veined) is the front door (on singing hinges) to a nest of deciduous feathers.

Tracheally vestibular; the esophageal slide down the bannister.

2

Histaminic prehistory. The octave-coupling left lung hisses an oxygen-fraught aria. Nest-building a pigeon-toed deliberation between interpleural histrionics and cardiac placidity (predictably).

3

Ridiculously nidicolous. The nest pecking-order a lobar-duet on the lowest scale: Niche-bullying. Gular-fluttering foundation.

When the bough breaks the bird-cradle is an airfoil foiled by air. Leaf-defeated bronchiole tree. Arpeggio of shallow breathing. Broken birdsong.

Three-Note Wing Chords...

 1
of Irruptive
Bronchial-
Tree
Nesters.

Cartilage
architecture.
Acoustics

 2
of sticks
and ligature,
membrana

tympaniformis,
variable-

 3
sweep
syrinx.

Oscine-
swing.

4

Passing-through
Passerines.
Stinging

wind,
Wax-

winging
hiatus.
Migratory

5

aperture.
Gap-
trajectory   (*hap
                        -hazard sparrow* ...).

6

Diagram

7

a diaphrag-
matic
absence.

Lung-

excursion,
peripatetic
trip-

8

switch.

Tseee-
    tseee-
       tseee-

pitched
pulmonary-

9

circuit-

broken

passage.

Lore: 4 (swoop)

Traverse the transverse arytenoid muscle. Aryepiglottic fold, corniculate tubercle, cricoid cartilage: swoop from larynx to the three-lobed amphitheatre.

Air-chamber nidification. The right lung partitions into upper, middle, and lower lobes, each with enough space to accommodate numerous cavity-nesting birds.

Hold an ear next to an oscine-inhabited lung and hear an antiphonal calling, the advance and recession of ocean, birds in a burble of aqueous-suspension.

Grus canadensis

1
Long
guttural
clatter.

Coiled
trachea.

Pneumatic
antiphonal
dance.

2
Lungs

an open marsh,
fenland, quagmire
of low gurgle and iron-
oxidized aspiration.

3
Sandhill Crane.
Spark bird,
bird that

burst
into the broncho-
pulmonary
decibel.

4

Shallow-
bend
maracas. Ribs

an anatomical
percussion.

Rattling
alveoli (breath

pebbles
the shoreline,
a line of un-

hatchable
eggs)

5

Hollow

bone

intubation.

6

Eye
the epiglottis,
then eyeball

the distance
from dry lands
to wetland.

Lore: 5 (agonist)

The wandering, halting warble of the Evening Grosbeak. The male of the species with a distinctive yellow flash extending from the base of its beak over the eyebrow towards the back of its head.

A reed-like fluticosone singing. Irregular summer laggard. The long-term corticosteroid song less clearly articulated.

Bronchodilators increase the bird-flow. Beta-agonists arouse an adrenalin of upperwings; primaries and outer tail feathers sputter the nest. The horizontal fissure issues a shrill *clee-ip clee-ip*.

Lore: 6 (pluvial)

1

Spish the song into sight. Sonogram a vertebration of short
tripping trills. Bobolinks. Wide-ranging pitches. Tallgrass, high-
note, swish-hitters.

2

Wishful singing. Pleurally plural. With the syrinx located at
or near the junction of the trachea and lungs some birds can
produce two distinct notes simultaneously.

3

Sturnella neglecta ("little starling") Tin whistle dipped in liquid
Wistful. Fluty flying *who-who are you?*

Meadowlark nebulization. Flaring nares. Between maxilla and
eye a goldenrod-tipped mist. Pluvially orchestral. Sparrowful.

Flight Song of the Old World . . .

1

Respiratory
Tract.
Ascend
the alveolar

ridge where tongue
-tip invokes Song

Sparrow,
chi-
chip
Chipping

2

Sparrows,
Wood
Warblers

warbling
water.
Aer-

o

-dynamic
swim up

3
the laryngeal
stream.
Water-
winging-

it flight
of the
dumb un-

founded
sound-
tract.
(Respiratory

4
intractability.)

5
Pulmonary
dialysate:
Ante-

diluvian
filtration (out

with the old
    and in
with the older),

lungs in-
filtrated

6

by House
Sparrows
(saggital-

narrow
passage, O_2
bypass).

7

*Passer
domesticus*
—200 million

year old flight-
path of old
soul-dead

air, glottal

8

stoppage,
glosso-

pharyngeal
ballistics.
Old World air-

9

balloon, inter-
clavicular

ballast,

feather-
light
flight.

Lore: 7 (aspect ratio)

Jizz of airborne lungs: venturi tube trachea; cul-de-sac lift/drag ratio; emphysematic airflow.

Pluck pterylography. The leading edge of the inferior lobe might be likened to that of the wings of the *Perdix perdix* or the *Bonasa umbellus*.

Aspect ratio of the lungs closer to that of a bird with shorter, broader wings, e.g. a variety of Grouse, than that of, say, a Swainson's Hawk, with longer, narrower wings.

Almost Migration . . .

1
of the Half
Collapsed
Flight-

Depleted
Lung.

2
Rib-pleated
concertina,
back and forth

windpipe
ambivalence

. . . debating oxygen as form . . .

3
Order
Strigiformes:

Barrel-chested
disputations.
Single-

lobed Snowy
Owl opus
(new snow-

4

soundless).
Pneumo-

5

thoracically
prone
Burrowing

Owl reverb.
Quickquickquick

False-
winged,
false

6

vocal cords.
Faulty
pneumatics.

Athene cunicularia:
Lung-squatter,
oxygen-borrower.

Fossorial.

7
Burrow
into feather
cortex, context

of fossil-
instinct,
migration

-cumbersome
bone. Lung-

8
lumbering.

Primordial
air (Jurassic

flight).

Lore: 8 (pop.)

Breadth of the lungs is such that the superior lobe bronchi comprise a vascular forest sustaining a population of typically ground-nesting White-Throated Sparrows, abundant in the bronchial ecozone from late spring to early autumn.

Chunky on perfunctory glance little-brown-jobs albeit with yellow branches of fire flitting off supraloral to middle lobe bronchus to inferior lobe bronchus. Alight and ascend. Alight and ascend. *soooo seeee dididi dididi sooo seeee dididi dididi.*

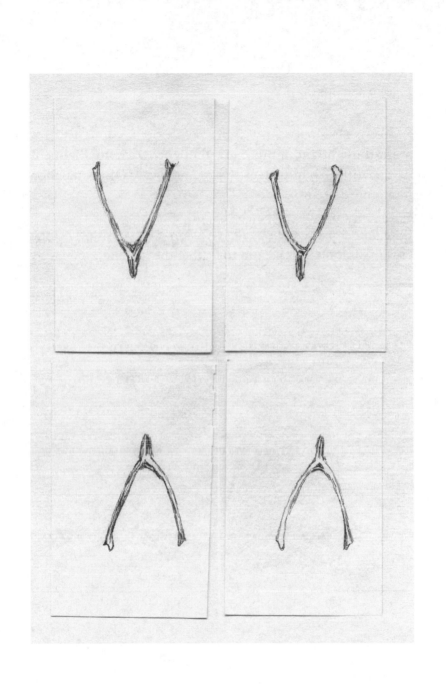

Lore: 9 (wishbone)

Merrythought and more merrythought. Oscinine flights of oxygenation. Song pierces the ozone layer; O_3 solmization (triatomic do-re-mi).

Furculaic optimism (clavicle fusion and wishin'). Bone pneumatisation. Epithelium to feather the landing.

Where the Neck Ends

The median lethal dose of tongue equal to its root's reach to the mediastinum. Down the throat and over the edge.

Hack the nasal labyrinth. Gravity. A back-smack. The blood/ brain barrier a gag reflex away. The chokepoint

is hackly and vocabular. Articulable but for hackles.

Where the Neck (really) Ends

Geography and water-depth coalesce in a corridor wide enough
for a pool-noodle. Lung and lung take a holiday. A trip down
the slick slipping synovial slide. Seaside is obsessive syneresis

. . . *glairy,*

like the white of an egg. Breath tripping up in a slippery diphthong.
The causeway a separation of sun and albumen. Long muscle
of the neck the line where swash meets swallow. Pool-noodling
uprush.

Cervical Vertebra Variation

Syringes crescendo incrementally. Segmental sound drift. Rostrum-gist shifts from leading edge to trailing. Feathers shed antithetically (*molto* molting melodeon).

Song of suction bellow and reed. Seven-process processional (one spinous, two transverse, four articular). Song of rachis and foramen. Spinal chorus.

Cervical Vertebra Variation 2

C2. Axis. Song cycle symphysis. The second cervical vertebra a pivot on which the air changes direction. Rotating wave

of Warblers. Palm Warbler's 6-plume repetition. Yellow Warbler's variable *sweet-sweet-sweet*. Caudal draft.

Cervical Vertebra Variation 3

Backward fold the cervical atlas. The spinal incunabulum articulates the isochronal loral line. Hollow bone archaeology. Canarygrass reed, elemental cannulae, transitional fossil thoracentesis (*Pulmonarius lithographica*). Cryptic

Archaeopteryx. Air-swindler. Non-bird bird. First flight

fires the neural arch. Trachea-crammed turning radius (mesotarsal ankle joint notwithstanding). Windpipe fipple, stippled hum (hyoid hymnody). Os sacrum. Sacral canal. Holy bone.

Ribcage Invention

1

Disarticulate the pectoral girdle. A wing-shaped dorsal-blade, the scapula scrapes by on a tune between humerus and collarbone.

2

Percuss the thoracic cage.
Clavicula: the little key that unlocks the door.

3

Scale the trailing rib edge. Rattle the bars. Below the anterior scalene the first ribs radiate from the manubrium in a high-perching arch . . .

Lore: 10 (rib)

Curve-bone tablature. Light-organ luthier. Costal cartilaginous tonewood.

A variable geometry. The major rib scale can ascend into fast flapping flight with the rip-opening wingbeat of a Needle-tailed Swift, or vibrate in place at the pollinating frequency spectrum of a Ruby-throated Hummingbird (multiflorous vocal waves).

Thoracic soundboard. Sternocostal soundhole (gladiolus rose). Inferior umbilicus plectra (display feather picking).

Floating Rib #11

1

Costae
fluitantes:
vertebral-

ethereal.

Bone
potion.

Cartilage
nectar.

Single-
faceted
hum.

2

(*Archilochus*
colubris.)
Anchorless.
A

down-
ward
legato

slur,
liquid,
a lig-

ature . . .

3
Dip di-
graphically.

(Bifurcated
sipper.)

Reed
to the needle

billed mouth-
piece. Foot-

spinning
pollinator:
Trochaic

4
Trochilidae.
(Evolutionary air

5

convergence,
thrum
strung
some-

6

where between
bird and bee:

7

Wing-
chime
chimera,
humming
hybrid-
vibratory.)
Trumped-

8

up *Apoidea*
signature song.

(Verb-ether
vocalism—
flower-kisser,
myrtle-imbiber,
ornithophilous rib-

inscriber.)

Hummingbird

1

Deep-keeled. A nickel's weight of charm and troubling. Airway territoriality. Pendulum arc bronchus flit. (Left, right, two-step flight.) Ventral symmetry.

2

Vocal fold ventriculus: hover assimilates hum. Tin ear tune an agonistic buffer.

Buzz note vocalization. Wing-box stammer. Stuttering chase call.

Hummingbird 2

1

Three-gram refraction. (Pulsatively breathtaking.) The jewel-necked vocal nexus a complex harmonic of nectar and reflecting. Wings fan flashes of fire. Rapid

hovering exhalations.

2

Exhilaration of capillaries. Song sung Audubonic. Lyrically alveolaric.

3

Color flutters three hundred breaths a minute the lungs hum red. Glittering fragments. Vignetting gems.

Hummingbird 3

1

Contradiction in terms of feet. Short-syllable Apodiforme.
Choriambulatory chorus. Humming carbuncle. Tongue to the
trumpet blossom. Flame-licked. (Ruby-tipped stylus.)

2

Tap tap the bronchiole tree. Deoxygenated orchestral. Red sap
surfs surfactant. Sip, hover, slip

through windpipe and reed. Sound peregrination.

3

Elliptically migratory. Follow the floral artery. Flight strung
with Paintbrush, Blazing Star, Torch Lily. (Bloom synchronicity.)
Crimson stung metabolic.

Lore: 11 (cleft)

Pulmonic harmonic. Syringeally sympatric. Converging venti-
latory ventriloquy.

Two or more birds producing similar vocalizations and the
visceral and parietal pleura vibrate at a frequency of oscillation
high enough for feathers to unzipper and leaves to turn Yellow
Warbler and fly. Notes zing from lung through the infundibular
cleft into the middle ear of the forest canopy.

Lore: 12 (midrib)

Arboricultural aerodynamics. Botanical flight patterns. The musically rattling Snow Buntings leave only a whoosh of air and feet perched holographically. Flight

in three dimensions. Concentric suspensions

of green. Small space photosynthesis. A concise ecology. A forest hovers in a single word: *Canopy*. Holophrastic. The origins of shelter an interference of light and dendrology.

Esophageal Hiatus

1

Count coaxial cartilage rings up the air channel. The utmost uppermost point is the pulmonary canopy.

A hole in the oscine layer is a study in tracheometrics. Windpipe orchestra. Woodwind bronchial forest. The voicebox? Flocculent. All utterance

scansorial.

2

Notes are the things with feathers. Call and release. Hum-tones in antigravitational flight. The well-tempered subclavian avian veins its way to the first rib. From neck to diaphragm the phrenic nerve is a Strat string waiting to sing. The stratosphere

utter color: ruby-gulleted, rose-torsoed, yellow covert sun with white scapulars, dappled.

Lore: 13 (shadow-decoy)

1

Nestling sostenuto. Ventilatory perfusion. Sound lingers then leaves the nest percutaneously. Acoustical porosity.

2

Countersong sung pneumomnemonically. Lush pelagic lungs. Sponge tissue spun with fowl grass and goose feather. Down-lined gosling-chambers. Hollow allure.

3

Lung Shadow Decoy. Lung Confidence-Decoy. Lungs lure the nectarivoracious. The wet-nesters, nest-robbers. Mimes. Mimics. Song-thrust, song-throttle.

Tally

1

Crosshatch the cardiorespiratory system in wing patterns one through nine. Invent an inventory.

1.1

(Hyperinflation inveracity.) Twelve shelves of thoracic sacs. Thirty-two short-winged variations of warble. The same six liters of call and response.

1.2

Biodiorama. The Life Lung List a drama of chest cavity and decoy. 3-D oxygenscapes. Breath-escaping scrape-nesters. Airway architectonics.

1.3

Woodpecker the manubrium. Bill bevel. Chisel-tipped. Red-shafted Flicker picklocks the thorax.

1.4

Big Thermal Year: vociferous wind box; wheezing squeeze box; lobe resonance box lyre.

1.5

Falsetto and feathers.
Lies and alula.

2

Brindle flash. Patchy anatomy. Invariably Thrush viral-pitch. Multicellular rush. Hush in the lung apex.

2.1

Sub-sing a suspensory ligament. Lingula interlude. Cardiac notch intermezzo.

3

Decrescendo Quack Series. (Iambphibious dabbler.) The submerged lung subnarrative flush with mallemuck muck, Sedge seed, Duckweed, Western Dock. (A mixed mixwood bag.) Air-pocket riparian.

3.1

Decrescendo Quack Series. Air-pocket riparian. Walking bass line catch basin. Rain-postured. Basal haze. Bronchospasmodic backwash batters the soft palate. Flip

the epiglottal emergency flap.

3.2

Decrescendo Quack Series. Flip the epiglottal emergency flap. Leaky lung-surround. Sound collapse. Spatch-cock the thorax. Pump the sump lung.

4

Post synch the syrinx. Pitch-hover the eleventh rib perch.

Sternal section insurrection: Movable rib scaffolding. (False rib solfeggio.) Floating notation.

4.1

Sotto voce oscillations. Whisper song. Song sunk sub respiratory.

4.2

Bird-surge virtuosity. (O oscine. O solo.)

Lore: 14 (mirror call)

Quick-striking bittern with a bill like a clapper. Head-bobbing rhythm-keeping Rock Dove. Rapid-tapping sapsucker, red-naped, nasal. Birds hitting below the belfry and lungs

are two-octave carillons. Fan-arteried. Campanulate. The left pulmonary veins carry a 25-bronchi clarion from the left lung back to the heart. Ventricles in a mirror dance of call and call and call and call...

Notes and Acknowledgments

In "Three-Note Wing Chords" the phrase "a haphazard sparrow" is from Will Alexander's poem "Provision for the Higher Ozone Body," from *Above the Human Nerve Domain*, Pavement Saw Press, 1998.

The line "debating oxygen as form," in "Almost Migration," is from Will Alexander's poem "Inside the Ghost Volcano," also from *Above the Human Nerve Domain*.

In "Where the Neck (really) Ends," *glairy, like the white of an egg* is part of Henry Gray's (*Gray's Anatomy*) description of synovial fluid. See Bill Hayes' *The Anatomist: A True Story of Gray's Anatomy*, New York: Ballantine Books, 2008.

———

Poems published here have previously appeared in *Conjunctions*, *Contemporary Verse 2*, *Matrix*, *New American Writing*, *Prairie Fire*, *The Capilano Review*, *Web Conjunctions*, and in the anthology *The Arcadia Project* (Ahsahta Press).

I am grateful for funding from the Canada Council for the Arts and the Saskatchewan Arts Board.

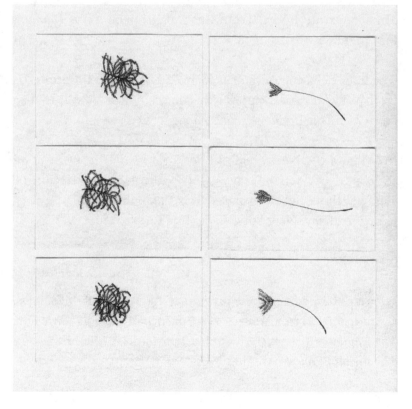